Ramadan Rhymes: Nursery Rhymes Colouring Book

Elizabeth Lymer (text; design)
Kim Reimann (illustrations; design)
Sandy Quigley (illustrations)
Aisha Davies (text)

Mindworks Publishing
Copyright © 2015 Elizabeth Lymer and Mindworks Publishing

Published by Mindworks Publishing,
Missouri City,
TX 77489

mindworkspublishing@gmail.com

Ramadan Rhymes videos can be streamed free of charge and without advertisements via the 'Elizabeth Lymer' YouTube channel at http://www.youtube.com.

D1401017

Ramadan Rhymes

Nursery Rhymes Colouring Book

Ramadan Rhymes
Nursery Rhymes Colouring Book

By Elizabeth Lymer (text; design), Kim Reimann (illustrations; design), Sandy Quigley (illustrations) and Aisha Davies (text)

Order of Nursery Rhymes

Oh Ramadan (Frederic Weatherly's 'Danny Boy' to the tune of the 'Londonderry Air')

It's The Month Of Fasting (I'm A Little Teapot)

Listen, A Mu'athin (I'm a Little Teapot)

Before Dawn Starts (The Queen of Hearts)

When It's Ramadan (The Wheels on the Bus)

Muslim Women And Men (See-saw Margery Daw)

'Azza Atkins (Jennie Jenkins)

Ramadan! (Hot Cross Buns)

We're Fasting, We're Praying (It's Raining, It's Pouring)

Muslim, Muslim, Keep Your Fasts (Horsey, Horsey, Don't You Stop)

Laa ilaaha ilallah (Old MacDonald Had A Farm)

Allah's The Forgiving (Incy Wincy Spider)

Hicham, Hicham, Drinking Zamzam (Mary, Mary, Quite Contrary)

Read, Read Al-Qur'an (Row, Row, Row Your Boat)

The Messengers (A Wise Old Owl)

To Allah I'm Grateful (I'm A Little Teapot)

'Eid-ul-Fitr (Bobby Shaftoe)

Celebrate, Celebrate 'Eid Today (Pat-a-cake, Pat-a-cake, Baker's Man)

Oh Ramadan

(Frederic Weatherly's 'Danny Boy' to the tune of the 'Londonderry Air')

Oh Ramadan, that month, that month, is calling,

To hearts of hearts, and deep within our minds,

Sha'ban's soon gone; we'll all be busy striving

For Him, for Him, to read and know His signs.

SubhanAllah, that month opens His Mercy,

And His forgiveness waits for me to plea,

I know my life exists because He made me

To worship Him, for worshipping will set me free.

But for this month, I know I'd be a failure,

Only through grace, I gratefully succeed

To see Him wait for me to seek His pleasure,

To pray always, in comfort and in need.

So bismillah, I'll bow, prostrate, and cry tears,

And I will ask Allah to quell my fear,

This Ramadan, I'll read His words and He'll hear,

And by His will, if He does will, He'll keep me near.

It's The Month Of Fasting

(I'm A Little Teapot)

It's the month of fasting: Ramadan,
The third pillar of Islam,
Charity and prayers form the programme,
And reciting the Qur'an.

It's the month of reading: Ramadan,
It's the month of the Qur'an,
Signs of truest guidance sent to man,
First revealed in Ramadan.

It's the month of praying: Ramadan,
Try to pray the most you can,
On the night of Qadr really cram,
While Allah sends next year's plan.

Listen, A Mu'athin

(I'm a Little Teapot)

Listen, a Mu'athin, loud and clear,
Hear him calling in your ear,
Time to come to Masjid, do you hear?
Come for Jama'at Salah here!

Ho Tally Tally

(Hey Diddle Diddle)

Ho tally tally!

Noor, Hicham and 'Ali

All sight the Ramadan moon;

The happy friends cheer

To see it up,

And intend to be fasting quite soon.

Before Dawn Starts

(The Queen of Hearts)

Before dawn starts
We prime our hearts
To fast for the whole day;
We look on charts
For when dawn starts
And stop suhoor and pray.
Iftar time starts
As day departs –
At sunset fasting ends;
Our mealtime starts
With grateful hearts
For all that Allah sends.

When It's Ramadan

(The Wheels on the Bus)

When it's Ramadan we fast and fast,
Fast and fast, fast and fast,
When it's Ramadan we fast and fast,
All day long.

When it's Ramadan we eat suhoor,
Eat suhoor, eat suhoor,
When it's Ramadan we eat suhoor,
Just before dawn.

When it's Ramadan we eat iftar,
Eat iftar, eat iftar,
When it's Ramadan we eat iftar,
When the sun's gone.

And in Ramadan we pray and pray,
Pray and pray, pray and pray,
And in Ramadan we pray and pray,
All night long.

When it's Ramadan we fast and fast,
Fast and fast, fast and fast,
When it's Ramadan we fast and fast,
All day long.

Muslim Women And Men

(See-saw Margery Daw)

Muslim women and men,

United with boys and girls fasting;

Eat nor drink from the dawn to sunset,

Obeying the Lord Everlasting.

'Azza Atkins

(Jennie Jenkins)

Oh, will you eat bread, oh my dear, oh my dear?
Oh, will you eat bread, 'Azza Atkins?

No I won't eat bread,
'Cause I'm fasting instead.
I'll strive for a
Bismillahi,
Laa ilaaha ilallahi,
Ramadan, to guide me.

Fast, fast, 'Azza Atkins, fast!

Oh, will you eat cheese, oh my dear, oh my dear?
Oh, will you eat cheese, 'Azza Atkins?
No I won't eat cheese,
'Cause I know Allah sees.
I'll strive for a bismillahi, laa ilaaha ilallahi, Ramadan, to guide me.
Fast, fast, 'Azza Atkins, fast!

Oh, will you eat meat, oh my dear, oh my dear?
Oh, will you eat meat, 'Azza Atkins?
No I won't eat meat,
'Cause I don't want to cheat.
I'll strive for a bismillahi, laa ilaaha ilallahi, Ramadan, to guide me.
Fast, fast, 'Azza Atkins, fast!

Oh, will you eat date, oh my dear, oh my dear?
Oh, will you eat date, 'Azza Atkins?
No I won't eat date,
'Cause I know I must wait.
I'll strive for a bismillahi, laa ilaaha ilallahi, Ramadan, to guide me.
Fast, fast, 'Azza Atkins, fast!

Oh, when will you eat, oh my dear, oh my dear?
Oh, when will you eat, 'Azza Atkins?
I will break my fast
When the day has passed.
I'll strive for a bismillahi, laa ilaaha ilallahi, Ramadan, to guide me.
Fast, fast, 'Azza Atkins, fast!

Ramadan!

(Hot Cross Buns)

Ram-a-dan! Ram-a-dan!

Girls are fasting, boys are fasting,

Ram-a-dan!

Be good while you fast and read and read Qur'an,

Girls are fasting, boys are fasting,

Ram-a-dan!

Ramadan!

(Continued)

Ram-a-dan! Ram-a-dan!

Mums are fasting, dads are fasting,

Ram-a-dan!

If you cannot fast feed someone if you can.

Mums are fasting, dads are fasting,

Ram-a-dan!

We're Fasting, We're Praying

(It's Raining, It's Pouring)

We're fasting, we're praying,

And, "Bismillah," we're saying,

We mention Him in everything,

For He is the One we're obeying.

Muslim, Muslim, Keep Your Fasts

(Horsey, Horsey, Don't You Stop)

Muslim, Muslim, keep your fasts,

Straighten your path while Ramadan lasts;

Be good at night and do good all day,

Let Islam improve your way.

Laa ilaaha ilallah

(Old MacDonald Had A Farm)

Laa ilaaha ilallah!
Praise Allah alone!
Muhammad is His Messenger,
By him we were shown:
To praise Allah here
And praise Allah there,
Here we praise, there we praise,
Everywhere we praise Him,
Laa ilaaha ilallah!
Praise Allah alone!

Laa ilaaha ilallah!
Praise Allah alone!
Muhammadur rasool Allah,
By him we were shown:
To praise Allah here
And praise Allah there,
Here we praise, there we praise,
Everywhere we praise Him,
Laa ilaaha ilallah!
Praise Allah alone!

Allah's The Forgiving

(Incy Wincy Spider)

Allah's the Forgiving,

Generous and Just,

Merciful Judge

In whom we put our trust.

He can forgive us

And guide us the straight way,

So let's turn and repent to Him

Sincerely everyday.

Hicham, Hicham, Drinking Zamzam

(Mary, Mary, Quite Contrary)

Hicham, Hicham, drinking Zamzam,
How do your evenings go?
With nafl Salah, Qur'an, and du'a,
For only Allah to know.

Hicham, Hicham, drinking Zamzam,
Why do you hope and fear?
All night your care is constant prayer –
Might Layat-ul-Qadr be here?

Read, Read Al-Qur'an

(Row, Row, Row Your Boat)

Read, read Al-Qur'an

Anywhere you are:

Heavenly, heavenly, heavenly, heavenly

Word sent from Allah.

The Messengers

(A Wise Old Owl)

The Messengers that walked this earth,

All lived the only way of worth:

To worship One Lord every day,

Sure that this life's a test, and not just play.

'Eid-ul-Fitr

(Bobby Shaftoe)

'Eid-ul-Fitr is today,
Let's dress up and go and pray,
Later on let's eat and play,
Happy 'Eid-ul-Fitr!

'Eid-ul-Fitr's full of fun,
It's a joy for everyone,
Thank Allah our fasting's done,
Happy 'Eid-ul-Fitr!

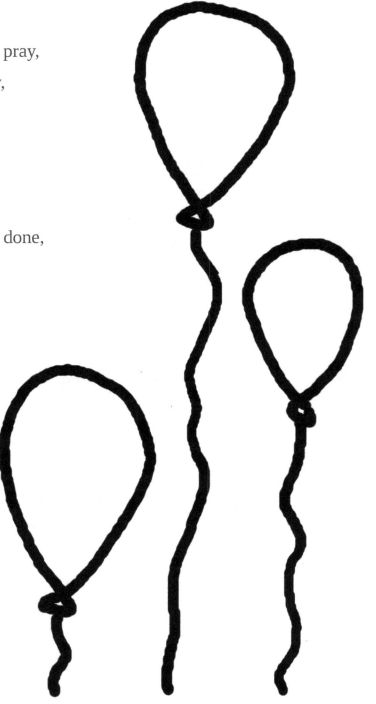

To Allah I'm Grateful

(I'm A Little Teapot)

To Allah I'm grateful, 'Eid is here,

"'Eid Mubarak" in my ear,

And "Saha 'Eidek" with happy cheer –

Love that Muslims share is clear.

Celebrate, Celebrate 'Eid Today

(Pat-a-cake, Pat-a-cake, Baker's Man)

Celebrate, celebrate 'Eid today,

Fasting has finished and food's on its way.

Cook it, and share it, and eat it with joy,

Allah provides food for each girl and boy,

For each girl and boy, for each girl and boy,

Allah provides food for each girl and boy.